High Spirits

Also by Paul Mitchell:

Matters of Life and Faith (essays) (2021)
We. Are. Family. (novel) (2016)
Standard Variation (poetry) (2014)
Dodging the Bull (short fiction) (2007)
Awake Despite the Hour (poetry) (2007)
Minorphysics (poetry) (2003)

High Spirits

Paul Mitchell

PUNCHER & WATTMANN

First published in 2024
Published by Puncher & Wattmann
PO Box 279
Waratah NSW 2298

info@puncherandwattmann.com

NATIONAL
LIBRARY
OF AUSTRALIA

A catalogue record for this book is available from The National Library of Australia.

ISBN   9781923099159

Cover design by David Musgrave
Printed by Lightning Source International

Contents

More Skills for Living 9

Panther 10

Psalm 19b 14

The Sun Moved to a Supplementary Position 15

Sermon on the Institution 17

Central Questions 19

And That's the Over 20

The Lowest Common Denominator is the View from the Top 22

Dead People I Know 28

Enlightenment 30

Marking Mark's Discovery 31

Iconostasis 33

Weekend Warriors of the Apocalypse 35

Morning, on the Road 38

Process Theology (a-c) 39

The Birth of Sophia 42

Snap Your Pencils in Half 44

Koans for the Young 45

Another Scene from a Marriage 47

Bootscooting in Paris 48

First Day of Holidays 50

Three on the Tree 52

Screen Play 53

Inception 59

The Movie Snatches 60

Letter to Franz Kafka 62

To Sleep or Not to Be 64

Portrait of What Came Next (Or) 65

Funereal 66

Portrait of Departure 67

Death of a Sparrow 68

Song in the Key of Beginner's Mind 69

For Jo, with tenderness and strength

More Skills for Living

Never let them see you're
hurting or let them
see you're trying
not to let them see. You're hurting?

Okay. Cue '90s alt rock anthem.
Let them watch you mouth the words.

That buzzing sensation in your back
is the rain on your umbrella
and a man you barely know
on the train   you fight
to find what it is
that men talk about. You both forget.
Another skill for living.

Panther

Addiction is an adaptation. It's not you − it's the cage you live in.

Johann Hari

I'm building you another cage.
Don't tell me where
to construct it. I'd only listen.

Growl on, grow up:
how do you like these
bars? Tasty, gritty? Blood
and gristle are your doing

marrow is up and singing
rooftops yours to tip toe across

and I'll tell no one
where you're sleeping.

Ha, just like hell
keeps a secret.

*

You were so cute
rolling on a lounge room floor
          chasing bales of human hair

in front of the fire.

I loved your sabre sweet
smile and eyes that stared

with Rilkean precision.

*

Ah, the growling in the grass
beneath my lungs move:

stay still, shoot me
          your stare says
the hill I'm climbing leads
to tightening stomach muscles

and your footprints
enlarging with every two steps
I take backwards into your arms.

*

Why pretend to sit behind me
as I comb my hair in the mirror?

Forget the eye roll and teeth bare
the anyone could tickle your tummy
purr: that mirror is a lake

and paw prints line the shore.

*

You study your prey: two gazelles
drinking by a lake's edge, red wine

or water, what does it matter?
More paw prints on the bar floor

are all the gazelles will see
as we wrestle til we're ghosts.

*

You're acquainted with the lord
of the jungle? But you don't seem
the slightest afraid. Neither am I

when the jungle's cooling
and the wind has fallen.

Then, it's true, you can lie
beside a campfire while I
tell stories of you, the kitten.

*

I imagined you old just now.
Barely a sack of bones by a dry

riverbed. You were, of course, alone.
You were, additionally, scraping

in my stomach for clues on how

to once more swallow leftovers

of my life before I've eaten.

Psalm 19b

Let me stand at a door that opens to ocean
ride on an orca under water, then up and out of it
leaping. Let me call to forests a name they've forgotten
their leaves breathe a breath from the mouths
of all children. Let me dive from a mountain
despite fear of falling, let the snow that I fly through
be skin that I land in. Let me river the windows
on skyscraping offices while clouds get in shape
for a priceless economy. Headlights in traffic are eyes
full of wisdom. Let me get out of my car and walk
with the billions in a line that leads to a clifftop cottage,
it fits all of us, easy, we listen to the story of living
words like an ocean stood up in and opened.

The Sun Moved to a Supplementary Position

and earth at first denied responsibility
but when interviewed
gave a little ground.

The air we breathe, as always,
played to the crowd
said controversy was its in and out, and defining clause.

A statement from the ocean: current form was strong
          but the sun was expected to evaporate
all meaning.   Nothing

          about refining positions

just a flood
          of comments from trees, flowers, fields
and fountains.   Leaves fell under the spotlight.

          A new report from the sun came in: just block it out:
catch the first wave home, the ocean added.   Mountains

noted tyre tracks leading from where
the reef had been smelt of cordite
and petrol.   Gone cold.

The seasons pointed to downward facing,
wolves took a stretch   on behalf of all nature

until   those passenger pigeons

          darkened the nest of microphones
made a single, blink of the iris announcement:

Hail the new sky, clouded
in current affairs

Sermon on the Institution

I came to bring you church
and church in abundance.
Come to me all who are
heavy laden and I will give you church.
I am the way, the truth
and the church. No one comes
to the father but through those doors.

Even the very tiles on your
cathedral roofs are numbered.
Why then do you worry
over budgets? Is not your church
worth more than many NGOs
and sporting clubs?

And when you church
don't be like heathens
who seek me in sunlight and scrubland,
go into your plain-walled buildings
and close the door. Your heavenly father
knows what you do in secret
and will reward you. With a good church
so you can fold your hands in your laps.

Blessed are you who minister
for you will be called makers of church.
But woe to you who love
for you throw evangelistic tracts
into the wind and watch them flutter . . .

What is the kingdom of church like,
to what shall I compare it?

It is like a Moreton Bay Fig
that a man chopped to the ground
then used the wood to construct
a row of dog kennels.
Somewhere to sleep while the world howls.

Central Questions

Ghosts were given standing ovations
long before the curtain and this seemed fitting.
Everything did. The ocean folding back
to preserve our footprints on the sand
and the way cold eyes of geniuses you bedded
seemed to glow at sunrise. They left you

only fob watches and eyeglasses, adrift
on driftwood. It was then we agreed
we'd lost our balance, our thoughts
about balance and our desire to find
our centres, or to question why they were
where the edge of being was.

And That's the Over

his life a highlight reel
of brochure-clogged letterboxes
infinite Victa mowers growling

through cricket coverage
and cracks in the pitch
of voices in his head

framing summer in a
hostile mood in Echuca
or wherever sunscreen bottles

stare through sightscreens
with night vision and pressure
builds up at one end

while strike rates crinkle
cut shots are difficult
from scattered packets

of bushy branches
spinning turnstiles
to walk to the crease

of his life where he thought
every leg slip a sign
to bat for the Americans

especially mid-westerners
over anyone in an Akubra
as a snub-nosed

glovesman drank beer
from a mower catcher
for collecting ghost nations

the innings of his life
contained that classic shot
he was trying to make

the day he saw a sparrow
get hit high and fall dead
onto a neighbour's cricket-free lawn

The Lowest Common Denominator is the View from the Top

On beginnings and other attempts

I hoped for more than this
        it comes again and passes:
a total eclipse of the kitchen
        can't stand the heat   can't
stand at all.   All I want
        is a dry twig   in a damp tree

all I can do
is wave a hand behind me
in lieu of a rudder. All I know
        is I don't know

who speaks   or listens
when a child's toy phone rings

I pick up and ask who it is
a voice says I think you know

it's time to put down the phone.

If only I could say that what I want to say
is deeper than words – ring, ring:

phone number caught between my teeth
detergent poured from a laundry window
to wash my mother's wrists.

On becoming a man too slow for dancing

We waltzed in the early evening garden
seven days before we married. There were
fourteen years in raindrop spring petals
unborn children in our steps
a house that clutched our waists and a divorce
to lower our arms. I can't remember
if the music we danced to
was any more silent than this.

Snapshot from the First Circle

The world is not only like this
it stays like this. It makes a living
this way and won't be swayed
from its axis; it's how the world
turns and if there's gravity in that
statement it's intended. You want

miracles, clean air, clear horizons.
I've seen flowcharts and photographs
bumper stickers, but the world
makes out while the sun shines
and I stack hay in a hell cart.

On becoming a man too slow for dancing II

I really enjoyed our separated holiday together.
I wish I could have become a man sooner.

Don't know how to say this
it doesn't matter.

I regret everything.
And more.

Took wise counsel today.
And shut up for a while.

Do you know it's been seven years?
Yes, time and all that.

On becoming a man too slow III

Let me put it to you this way:
I never loved you and I always have.
I always loved you from the moment
you walked away and from the first time
I saw you I loved the way you left.

A meeting of sorted sorts

We're here to murder the twenty-first century
hooded men at my door announced. I was
unenthusiastic, but allowed them in
for tea and biscuits. It'd been a while
since I'd had company. And these guys
were at least clean. We talked for some time
at my kitchen table of belief, passion, progress
and duty. Causes, just or otherwise. The rest
of the morning, I'm afraid, got ugly.

Man too slow postscript

Everyone wants to know who
was to blame for the couple's break up.
No one ever asks who was to blame
for them staying together too long.

Full blast

Scorpion on mind's tongue claws rage within
and rage without and the world I've changed
leads to the bowels of some other prophet's
doomed re-entry to the craft without holy book
or holiday crowd in sight.

I use my coffin lid as a shield.

Get the jewels, shove the world and its hate crime
logbook in the back slip of your bum bag
and let's make for where the sun don't shine
the time is ripe, the apple is rotten and there's not
a single thing Denmark or Camelot have got
in common. Whenever the Golden Bough swings
we'll sell our mystery to the hornet's nest
of microphones, arrive with every reason
not to, with a thousand words that all say No
and refuse to code an app to click a button
to make billionaire prophets and presidents
of all of us. So if it's okay with you and everyone
I'm turning to it full blast with hammer raised
so nut nail crackers better get their soufflé on.

Notes on the disintegration

Our eyes, you see, are painted glass
we have a marble to leave in space
so we can make our mistakes
elsewhere: Ha! *Your* mistakes!

We sat down yesterday with the Pain
Minister. She told us to get a grip
on our magic once were wondrous

eyes and keep the future fires smokin'.
You have rest periods to come
between sewing each other's wounds,
she said. And by the way, I'm the only one
who can say I was here before the planet
rape scene you cut. We screamed:

wasn't that your speech, not our movie?
as we ate machine gun cones
in the back rows of operating theatres.

An anniversary of antipathy

I tried to text you ten times
but the words kept getting replaced
so blame the algorithms and my
biorhythms for someone saying
I wish there was *autocrat*
for my life.
Damn, it doesn't work ...

A final attempt

A constant saying
and unsaying continual rhythm
of broken in half-ness in time
to never was.

A good man haunts the world's supermarkets:

What I can tell you is that everything is continuing as normal
at Coles. The checkout girl who's more beautiful
than those advertised still doesn't realise she could play
a worse version of herself for quadruple the pay

and droop-faced men with organised beards,
astonished young women in grandma dresses
almost asleep in the baby aisle say, Nobody ever told us . . .

. . . oh, yes, we did, say oldies crouched to argue the toss
at the salad bar: the one-dollar one we had last week
or the two-dollar one that tastes too good for our weak hearts?
Speaking of artichokes: girls in hotpant active hip butt
huggers make too far grown silver hair in men's ears
stand straight as lines are long at auto-staffed checkout queues
and the hairy bloke waiting for smokes at the counter
no one gets served at is, you guessed it.

I leave with my checklist and the memory
I always get in the car park:

the last time I saw that guy alive
who died of a stroke at the airport
'cos people thought he was drunk
and didn't help, that same guy

who loved people of every shape
and colour in this supermarket life

who waved at me in the Coles car park
standing at the back of a Corolla Hatch
the same vehicle badge I'm putting
groceries in now. At least

we have that in common.

Dead People I Know

you're ice cubes too long in a freezer
and frost I can't get off
my windscreen even with boiling water

please explain
those crumbling yellow notes
at the back
of my filing cabinet

tell me too about black eyes
of fish in buckets

it would be too simple to say
stop calling me

as simple as forgetting
to say hello to you   I'd like to

analyse your dreams
assess them for lifelikeness
it's enough
you're silent
must you also be
resentful?   Or are you just forgetful?
You're not so proud of yourselves
now are you? Don't think for a moment

I don't know my bones
are your attempts
at memory

I know
it's too simple
to say you're alive in my heart so let me

simply say you're alive   you can't
trick me twice

Enlightenment

after Van Morrison's song, 'Enlightenment'

Enlightenment says the world's an illusion, but I wonder
about enlightenment's experience of war, attrition
and psychic pain, whether enlightenment's getting
a little ethereal about earthly existence. The last time
I felt oneness with the universe I was contemplating a tree
for twenty minutes and felt myself become the bright green
leaves and those leaves me. But enlightenment says that was
no less an illusion than the stabbing pain in my back
as my lifeforce was siphoned into a full-time job.
Enlightenment says both the job and my lifeforce
and even the stabbing pain are illusions. But I think
enlightenment is the illusion while everything else exists
to prove it doesn't. Still, who am I to question
enlightenment when just now my train passes
a giant black and white image of a Hindu Goddess
spray-canned on the rail bridge brickwork? I am,
according to enlightenment, thankfully, no one.

Marking Mark's Discovery

In the bar toilet thinking
I should ask my friend Mark
who I've been drinking with
what music he's been listening to lately
because tonight I'm conscious
how often I hog conversation
haven't been much of a friend to him
he's been a much better one to me.

So back at our booth with our beers set down
I ask *how* do you listen to music these days? He says
mainly on the iPod but I have Spotify on my laptop
and back in the toilet I'd already decided
to ask Mark if he'd heard of Mark Eitzel
because I'd been listening to his album
without pause – on my playlist
I can't flick past him, and my friend, like Eitzel,
has a British connection; well, Eitzel lived there
and Mark was born there, but I think Mark
will like Eitzel; he's literate and Cohenesque
so I ask Mark if he's heard of Mark
Eitzel and he says, "Mark Eitzel?"and I say,
"Yeah, I love him." And Mark says, "American Music Club
Mark Eitzel?" and I say, "Yeah, but I've only heard him solo"
and Mark says, "You know my best mate in England,
Paulo?" and I say, "Yeah, you've told me about him,"
but I don't tell Mark that whenever he tells me
about Paulo I get just a little bit jealous
as much because Mark is fifty-something and has
managed to maintain a best friend as much as
I'm not him. But it doesn't last long because I'm trying
to be the best friend I can, in the moment, like that one

in the toilet when I thought of telling Mark about
Mark Eitzel, and Mark tells me Paulo's favourite
musician is Mark Eitzel, and Mark adds he shouldn't be
surprised given my similarities with Paulo – my making poetry,
making music – but he says nothing of my name. I ask
Mark, "Do you like Mark Eitzel?" and Mark says, "You know,
I've never listened to him," and I say, "How can he be
your best mate's favourite and you've never listened
to him?" and Mark says it's because he's always had
this thing with Paulo where they respect each other's
music but can't cross music party lines: Mark
was a Bryan Ferry man, while Paulo was David Bowie's boy.

I'm not sure when I tell Mark that Eitzel's album's called
Hey, Mr Ferryman, but I sing the first two lines:
"The Ferryman who takes me to my rest/
he don't give a damn who's cursed or blessed."
Mark likes that, I tell him Eitzel became a Christian
then gave it up, and because we've both given up
a lot of what people think being a Christian means
we wonder what Eitzel gave up too, and Mark
tells me Paulo gave it up so maybe that's why
he likes Eitzel, and Mark says me and Paulo
liking Eitzel is a sign from somewhere, he doesn't say where,
that he should listen to him, shouldn't he, and I wish
I'd said Paulo would like that, or, Hey, Mr Ferryman
get on that boat, but I think I just said, "Yeah".

Iconostasis

Let's say it's the wink of sky and sea
or, if you prefer, land and river.

There, it's a surprise to find
what's needed is all you've been

not what you've done. Odd
also to find rabbits scaring

snakes to retreat, bared
teeth and bristled fur.

It might be a fold in time,
ripple of wind in arm hairs

before the touch of a loved one
already entombed. An empty

child's swing on a gum tree
to and fro, unoiled hinges

of birdsong. Where what
you say matters less than

why you say it. Let's not
get started on what's written.

Instead, let's think of it
as a hollow in a downed

dead tree where echidnas
are giving birth, the crest

of a wave before it crashes
and any amount of hidden

desert flowers before
storms unveil them.

That will be enough for us
to know and hold it

ripe in our hands, long
before we touch it.

Weekend Warriors of the Apocalypse

So, whatta ya been upta?
Oh, not much, cruisin round
gettin stuff done, waitin
for the great unveilin
of the saints at the end of time
that kinda thing . . .

Yeah, sounds good, I been
down at Bunnings, snags
were burnt, but I don't mind.

Yep, been there, got snagged
lookin for wood to build
a bobsled billy cart to hoon
the dunes when the great sands
come sweepin through the city...

Ah, yeah, give me the apocalypse
before Harvey Norman.

Nah, Go Get It While it's Hot!
Go!

Get the lawns done?
Yeah, I got em done, mowed
the bollards down and the tombstones
too: won't be needin them for bodily
resurrection and that . . .

What about the barbecue?
Cleaned it, ashes, cremations?

They're a bit harder, yeah, might need
a licensed contractor, fair bitta
repair the cells and stitch up
the DNA on those ones . . .

Anyway, I'll see ya down The Corner Hotel
or the Book of Revelation Station?

Yeah, mate, gotta potta gold
a golden ticket and trailer load
of leatherbound Bibles to give ya.
Slap em round like a New Idea
like a Who the Flamin Hell's
in Hell This Week Weekly.

All day Sunday and on til Christmas
Jesus, the decorations in the shops already?
And the winter's turnin to something or other
can't get me tomatoes to grow and the moon's
turned blood red, and I can't get those
scales from the dead fish outta me eyes!

Yeah, I hear ya: my body's a Jerusalem of injuries

Wife been good?
She's well, not ordained, but organised.

Yeah, gotcha, mine's the same. Loves a good
garden of eden at the drop of a fig leaf.

Can't argue with that.
Nah, ya can't.
Well, ya could.
But it'd do ya no good.

Right you are and a bucket of worms
for your turn to plant the seed of the gospel.

Gunna do a workin bee?
Yeah, wouldn't miss it for all the honey
and locust in your stink bomb beard, Johnny.
Onya.

Onya too, Pete.

Nah, look it's been
good to preach ya pants off
and sweet to see ya still got a head
on ya shoulders, old fella.

Catch ya by the river
with the fishermen, yeah.
Be a Christ load of us there, mate
we've been catchin 'em all night
and no sign of it stoppin anytime soon.

Morning, on the Road

Now I'm awake I'm walking the road to Emmaus
talking with you about who you are and who I'm not

and who I'm supposed to be. I can smell a barbecue

and I wouldn't mind a beer, but you say,
          "I can't just pull them out of the air;
miracles have a whole new meaning for me now."

 "They haven't much meaning for me," I say,
"except for waking up, enough to eat
          and someone to smile at."

"That's a lot," you say, and I can't disagree, and I admit

it's a little miracle, you and me walking the road to Emmaus
when I've never been near it

and I haven't managed to put my dressing gown on yet.

I'd say what you said to say goodbye, but you were gone
on the road to someone else's prayer.

Process Theology (a-b)

Process Theology (a)

I'm planning to write a poem tomorrow
it'll seem a lot like life.   Not quite mine

or yours
              or anything like ours

              just a life spent lying
under a tree on college grounds

staring through branches at the sun
because class was skipped, a soul was saved

and what else was there to do but listen
              to Brian Eno on cassette

'til sunset, marriage, childbirth and rapture?

Well, let's not get ahead of ourselves:

there was the fact the college grounds
              overlooked a cemetery

and the college motto was

Aedificamus in Aeternum.

We could, instead, get behind ourselves
recognise that when a Rubik's cube's
solved it should simply be

tossed in the air, so why not

      a soul that's saved?

There's little more to say
than this: tomorrow's
      life could be an improvement upon

today's poem. But today's does have something:

a line or two of
      the best future I planned.

Process Theology (b)

I am writing today a poem I planned to write
yesterday. It looks and sounds exactly
like my life: a cold, windowless office

at the back of a weatherboard shed.
A power saw cutting through the morning's
peace, the ticking of a novelty clock

my latest son bought for Father's Day
a pigeon, choking and chortling
traffic from six lanes the office walls

try to turn to ocean waves
and the thick glass on the door pane

working against every plane
Tullamarine takes in a day.

The computer stares at me
with a day's work inside
while I pen this into a foolscap

pad on a fool's errand to write
a poem that might outlast my life.

It looks exactly like this.

Process ~~Theology (c)~~

Today's poem has no good news
so go read your horoscope . . .

Nope? Max Dupain's bloke's lying
on the beach in sepia in a brochure

sticking out of a rack in the café
oblivious to the poem I based

on the image in two-thousand
that got published in *The Australian.*

Looking at me, Max's photo?
Inspiring me, Max's photo?

I recall it wasn't that photo
I based my poem on. It was

another Dupain. My inner critic
can't even get his artwork

in order. What hope the poet
sorting out the process?

The Birth of Sophia

You asked would she be
  a swathe cut through
grass blades
    or the view of spheres
before planets were made.

Before she could answer
three cold moons told her
all that's smooth is not a path.

You didn't know where

she began
and you ended

which is to say the sky
supplied her dreams.

(Never mind your sky was a bird
she worshiped at the altar of an egg.)

    She was millennia
dark in the worming
   mud patch of your garden
where she knew neither heart nor matter

   but you couldn't stop her being born
before the world's womb!

She made choice.

She was the undergarment of truth,
the slip of forgiveness,
she left herself crying at the altar
but walked with you
to the feast of the first born.

Do you see her, Living One, above you –
       she swoops from your fire, a bird in flame
healing our wounds in a blaze of words.

Snap Your Pencils in Half

It's not an exam you have to pass
or a test of patience:
         /how to row a boat without oars
across a sandbank/   okay, it's a bit
        repetitive

a daisy chain of ghosts stretched
between two oaks
in your darkening backyard.

But it's not a profit and loss statement
made at an accountant's lunch

nor a dream, memory or nightmare —
        the one
        where you didn't know the subject
        was on your curriculum
        and now —

it's neither exam nor test
nor three-part harmony from a choir
of essays.   It's like the place
where you get to watch yourself trying

        to figure out
where you are.   It resembles the last time

you pushed that boulder up the hill
to watch it crash back down   but it's more
like the day you thought you'd kiss the sky

then realised the earth would do.

Koans for the Young

∧

Just because ghosts don't exist
doesn't mean they can't
haunt you.

∧

When you're old
remind the younger you
that you don't like
what old people say.

∧

Once you realise you don't
know anything you'll know
you're no longer young.

∧

Imagine you're talking
to your younger self.
Now imagine that's me.
Luckily, I've got nothing
to say. Not to you, anyway.

∧

As you know, time
is only the same for us
because we're on this
planet. But when are you
reading this?

∧

A theory destroyed

is an angel shooting
a pop gun at a circus
lion projected on
a clown's behind.

^

God knows everything
except how to be
an atheist.

^

That dream you keep
having where you miss
your exam hasn't happened
yet. If it has, remember:
the answers are in koans
I've yet to write.

>

I had a final koan in mind
about the wind
but it was gone before
I had time to wonder
where it came from.

Another Scene From a Marriage

The morning doesn't start well: she says for breakfast
stop being such a bastard, and for morning coffee
you've got a PhD in Misogyny. I say that's a horrible
thing to say and I want an apology. She offers it
with a but, and a but, and a but you. I go to whatever
it is I'm doing and she goes to wherever it is she goes
and the issue we're arguing about isn't even
from our relationship but I guess it is now.

I leave my phone in the car and she calls me
on a friend's later and says I'm sorry
about this morning and I say it's okay
and she says it isn't really but maybe
I'm more qualified than she thinks to know
it's better if some things are still left to say.

Bootscooting in Paris

"The word itself is a musical sound" – Pierre Berace

Remember the lock bridge but not the water,
nor whether a *New Yorker* cartoonist cartooned it
permanently assailed by burly men with bolt cutters.
Remember, especially, we didn't buy a padlock
to lock to the bridge in lieu of our hearts.

Forget, like I have, the name of the lock bridge
but recall cheap cheese, expensive to our taste
cheap wine the same, recall the heat and sirens
the train to the ring we caught from the airport
with the beggar begging for Christians, at least,
to give him dollars they hadn't converted.

Remember the train to Versailles and the Sun
God – what were all those rooms for? I keep
getting it all mixed up with Venice, where we
decided we might divorce because you couldn't
endure another minute of me getting us lost

and we had to pay for a vaporetto to get us
to the train to Paris – for my virgine Parisean
experience – to visit the lock bridge, the tower,
the cheese and the arch – to forget to make love
(I remembered) because, you said, the heat
and our five-year-old and your fifteen-year-old.

"Why don't we go out dancing?" you said,
which is fine for you who tangos, foxtrots,
salsas and discos. I said, "What, bootscoot?"
because I'm Phil Collins with more hair,
back then, instead we visited Bastille, I think

you pointed at it, but I couldn't see what I
was supposed to, it was too dark
and my turning heart had stalled.

There were no yellow streetlamps
nor bedrooms with empty chairs
and paintbrushes forgone, but what about
that passing parade? The men in stockings,
those girls so tight beside them
frilly and follied, and how they
slapped their thighs when they saw us
pouting in Paris, down and out and danceless.

First Day of Holidays

Sometimes you just have to be
the person collecting shells
on the beach. The blue day
will be perfect. There'll be
nothing you can do about that.
As you collect, you'll consider
humanity's search for beauty
and perfection. You'll do
the usual wondering about
cultural preservation
in the presence of middens
and accompanying moonah.
Unseen species of seabird
will announce the necessity
of every migration, and you
will take off your shoes so
the rough shells slow you down.

Now you can feel how to see.

You'll think this is the perfect
beginning and that nothing ever
ends and all the rest of the mystical
hoo-ha you can neither predict
nor control. And so you will collect
your perfect shells and notice
one holds a mollusc that has
dried out and died in the sun.
And even this will be perfect, leading you
to reflect on the life
that grows in every death, that
resurrection is merely one of

many hopes, that every perfect
day, of course, must end. But
how about those sea shells, what
about that last breath of cloud
falling faithfully into the coming night?
And that final caramel curled shell your lover
delivered to your sandy hand as a gift.

Three on the Tree

Gold HG Holden Premier nineteen seventy-one
sedan with single dint on side door panel
installed a decent hi-fi in it played
Red Hot Chili Peppers on it took
fifteen minutes to warm up
each morning backed into a ditch
on the school run workmen
hauled it out with a winch.

Drove it drunk to a pub with mates
listening to Bee Gees Tragedy or something
bought it with the help of a mate who said
it's gold could see that and what he meant.

Cost three-thousand five-hundred
two years later needed money divorcee
dad on the wrong side of what
there's no right side of.

Sold it to a bloke who said
he'd put a new motor in it
mag wheels on it got three
thousand five-hundred for it.

Tired of being watched
wherever it went wanted to go
in cognito bought a Daewoo
Station Wagon didn't have to go
that far but did so sorry at least
let me show you the photos.

Screen Play

Scene One

      How long does it take to write a poem, how long
to live a life?   The poet

writes himself into a film

no one takes
the gun from the wall
in stanza one — or recognises
      all sun-filled gardens are open

for meditation but none for prayer.

      Take a shot of that shot if it triggers you.

Scene Two

Ah, Chekov's a gun, isn't he, but

      we could try a Black Panther
but I note

Rilke pacing back and forth. What about

a tiger? No, Blake's burning in anger at that simulacra.

      A stallion?

Please, don't matinee the audience's intelligence.

Listen, no one said
a poem
that showed its inner workings
would be easy, Malcolm, and there will be

no footnotes for you here or in history.

But endnotes?

Yeah, they've got the horror story Poeness

this poem's been looking for ...

Let's call it *The Great Dictator's Imitation Game*

and . . .

Scene Three

... strip him of his tiny moustache and military garb

(It takes ten minutes so far, Chekhov)

and drooping microphone. Rob him of everything
comic, Chaplain him, plant him deep in my
              metaphor

for a heart

inside the great, rarely opened treasure chest
at the centre of my simile for a soul

... Oh island in the sun, willed to me by my

Belafonte Donne

... Anyway, I'm a rock that feels no pain
has no room
for palm trees
or palms read
by Freud
dropping leaves
and coconuts to avoid looking
at those ballsy blokes kicking sand.

Scene Four

(sex scene)

In Physical Education, Year 12
I learnt about the sliding
filament theory and haven't
needed another metaphor since.

(Seventeen minutes and Chekhov
should be gulped in one shot
like a gun vodka drinker would).

Scene Five

That brings me to the Russians
and takes me away again.

Forget footnotes to Shakespeare
how about all the scribblers
are endnotes to Dostoevsky, himself
a parenthesis of Tolstoy?

(delete deleted scene)

underscore: DELETE

because

this is the scene
where Tarantino
would appear and say

"I've forgotten
how to write poetry. This is me

attending a workshop
with myself. Chekhov's gun
is a time limit
I've given myself to provide
an action film's ticking clock
which, unbeknown to readers,
stops at ____ minutes

after which I must go and teach

screenwriting."

(*Laughter from actors in 'studio audience'*)

Scene Six

Twenty-one minutes — no one gets out

of this poem alive, she cried, Jim.

But the real question is weather

The real sun, frying my fraying dome

will force me to stop this poem

before it reaches the conclusion

I can hear stallioning, tigering and panthering

up the hill toward me, where I stand, what

Naked?

No, I think that's good: imagine the indelible

mark this makes on you if you imagine

no, stop … undress now, *read* this naked …

(Oh, in the name of Scorsese!
Must be only ___ minutes to go)

The sun's too hot. The man meditating
has left the garden. The man praying
was never there

except in the mind of the poet
who yelled him umbilically into

Don't tell me how to read poems.

Don't tell me what a poem is.

Go home to the cinema.

(Screen turns black, credits roll
line endings
positioned ironically)

Inception

I am, of course, the thimble top thing
that's still spinning, but I go deeper,
three layers further, so tell me you can't
taste snow on my lips, feel my soaking
clothes or smell the air hostess's
breath. I've spent centuries waiting
in this empty hotel for you to come
and simply say hello. And now you're here

you want to smell some common sense
and logic. Okay, I could have imagined
larger weapons more often to ward off
dreamt-up enemies, and the circular nature
of dream and reality made two dimensional
models of both. But try looking at a Parisian
outdoor café the same way again
or the slow opening of an elevator door.

The Movie Snatches

Ralph Fiennes flies a single-engine plane
above the desert
and there's someone dead
in the cockpit
while Brad Pitt and Morgan Freeman
look haunted   walking

from room to room, Steve McQueen's on a motorbike
jumping a fence
and, plaster on his face, Jack Nicholson's
in '20s jazz age America

Brando says he could have been a contender
looks down and out

Another time he shouts up at a woman
hanging her head out a window

A pig runs mad through the outback
and a bunch of sheds fall over

while somewhere else
a bunch of sharks
fall out of the sky
and they're not happy

A woman sits in the jungle with gorillas
and Arnie and Danny are twins
who might be detectives

A lot of Mayans
kill the hell out of each other

in the jungle

while Hopper and Walken face off in a cabin
talking about who is a cantaloupe

Letter to Franz Kafka

Given your output, I'm sorry to write only a letter, but I have these Annual Reports to type, so time's an insect, attention spans and shelf-times shorter, and the Digital Age makes burning manuscripts impossible. What would you say to Brod now? Dismantle my hard drive? No, you'd have lived – medical science, etc. – and made a career decision: no interviews, no Writers' Festivals, just the dip and scrape of fountain pen in place of celebrity soundbytes. But we can't work on Annual Reports every year of our lives: Brod would have drafted you a Grant Application. Yet I'd love to read your Annual Reports for what they wouldn't have said so clearly.

Anyway, a *letter*. So some news: we fade, hair and pixels from photographs of photographs, held in trembling hands by a kindly Old Man, his fingertips yellowing. But this is not news for you. And what of the *yellowing*? All fingertips are dark and so, according to what the light from every open doorway told you, is the future.

Did Diamant read you a Yiddish version of the man whose barn and soul burnt the night he praised himself for his fortune? Sent to hell, that man asked for a drink of water from a saint. I'm sure you'd have told him, *That gate, my friend, was open, but I'm now about to close it* ... Like that man, after I read *The Trial* I thought I knew everything. But I couldn't explain it to anyone, *The Trial* or everything. So I write and write, dismantling myself, the Other, significance and sense.

Am I an insect or just a person of no consequence? Continual questioning makes me think I have consequence, but the consequence of that, you might have said, is this: *Who are you to say what I might have said?* But while I'm questioning, here's another: did you imagine a life without living?

We sweat, we die, we make ourselves eat our meals, we work, we die, we write and die and cough and forget our manuscripts. Seagulls bay for blood, insects smile in beds, and both dream of albatrosses, carrying stones to lands where no one writes Annual Reports, chips are spat on and children munch bugs for fun and don't exist, where even existence does not exist. And I, the I you left me with, takes strange comfort in the blank eyes of servants and maids in gold-plated suits and ties, insured against future losses, stock market crash test dummies, they're safe in the idea they're here, not in the Otherworld that both refuses them and to be.

Here, where money buys them, they scrap their souls, secure in the knowledge bargain bins are taken to the curb, but rubbish trucks won't arrive; they're driven by ghosts of ghosts who give each other respectful nods, who read and write burning manuscripts, while the idea of heaven persists, which surely must be hell for them.

Look, it's been a longer letter than I expected. I thought I'd stand a moment at your gate, ajar as always, light creeping through, as only light can, your voice tunnelling from the past: *It's cold, I'll close the gate* ... But you're telling lies. I'm going in, but now my finger's stuck. You'll have to tear it off to shut me out. Go on, do it: I know it's better to go through life without a finger than for my tongue to go up in flames.

To Sleep or Not to Be

I fall asleep to die or dream
my curtains call, their flap relentless
I am no longer who I've been.

The night will shorten, moon will beam
tide its prisoner, seaweed bound
I fall asleep to die or dream.

This bed that's held me since my teens
wants to toss me, blow my cover
I am no longer who I've been.

Don't wake me up, don't hold my hand
I'll build a mansion when I sleep
its ballroom plastic, flooring sand.

All my lost loves can fawn and preen
though a mirror holds what looks like me
I am no longer who I've been.

My blood has settled, sleep is mine
Or should I say I'm in the dark?
I fall asleep to die or dream
I am no longer who I've been.

Portrait of What Came Next (Or)

after Gerald Stern

What I failed to understand about a woman's body
turned out to be everything I needed to know
about bank accounts.

All the names I forgot from primary school
were later needed for signing on plane wings,
those skywriting bullies.

What I didn't know about onions was everything
I needed to feel about tiny gravestones in the rain
and nothing I needed to remember
about lipreading.

Coins that fell from my pockets in fistfights
were all the cymbal crashes I needed for typing
annual reports.

And what I thought was a baby's bonnet
was revealed to be my biography
written two-fisted by a baboon
crying for milkshakes and a PhD.

Funereal

In a room where my grandmother sits knitting
there's a dark clock. I cannot say
it's a grandfather, but I might say it's tall,
hunched over a newspaper, headlines
always summarising nineteen forty-three.

In this sitting room, my grandmother stands,
lays her wool and needles down
on a cushion for which she's knitting
yet another cover. Who wore them out

only the dark clock can tell as time and again
my grandmother pulls away from its arms.
"It's time," I say from the corner of the room
opening blinds so we can see outside

a black car, headlamps blinking on
off and on. My grandmother nods
and leaves the room and we would
both like to say the dark clock stopped
but nothing could be further from that room.

Portrait of Departure

Elderly couple, Sussex Street, Yarraville

Carried from their neatly clipped garden
like sleeping children carried from a party
asleep until bodies that held them
warm new beds, nodding one last approval

at their brick veneer, Greek columns,
creaking plum tree, aged fruit oddly ripened.
A windless autumn day at dusk
radio talks back, but its problems
are ludicrous. Lawns are watered, mown
and edged; it's cuppa tea in silence
that can only be conversation.

Green shade cloth screens their house
but they're carried to where green shade
is not required. They laugh at the memory
of green shade cloth, it takes the shape
of a belly dancer, spiralling to the beat
of talkback radio, her shimmied scarf draped
on their necks makes neither blush
but drags them from their directors' chairs
for a vigorous gardening session.

They're carried when they're ready
and not before. By a warm soft palm,
a caress and a whisper from
a cherubim statue: *It's time to go now*
where you've always been.

Death of a Sparrow

after A.D. Hope

O Silence, do you remember that sparrow
falling into my neighbour's front yard dead
at dusk? I passed as it made landfall

its lifelessness speaking of life;
numbering of feathers
and hairs on heads, a father's care.

But the sparrow still lay without its life
and I walked away with a photo
I didn't take; sepia puffed up breast
of air taken in and never let out.

On soft leaf buffalo grass alone
I left it, whispering proverbs and parables
until they fell in fertile soil that's kept
a sparrow's death alive these years.

O Silence, how many times I've longed
to sit on a nature strip and shout
of this burden. But day after day
I fold my wings and take to imagined skies.

Song in the Key of Beginner's Mind

In stillness at the kitchen table
before the school day
        think of Carver writing a poem
(at his kitchen table)
        while his children play. Or is that Dawe?
Definitely
not someone who knocks
        poetry with meaning and feeling

and senses.
I'm alone for the moment.   And still.

In this day,

        still playing with words, before

my child starts his day
surely wasting youth by being young.

        I remember mine:

I was not waving, hands
that broke the surface of grammar
were shark fins
and a mouth to eat the world

Epicurean of the heart I wanted to be
procrustean of the soul I became.

Now I hope to belong to what I long for,
but I'm still
        looking

for a way to lasso my life

While Eve
calls for Adam
do something, anything,
about these apples
falling from the fruit bowl.

**_*

And well may we say
breakfast is a good thing.
The muesli of morning news:
somebody's heartbreak
someone else's joy, a weather report
slick as the oil price.

And well may we say
clean teeth are a good thing
a son humming "I Still
Haven't Found What I'm
Looking For" - Dad, what
are you looking for?

Coffee.
Hot.
Everyone

alive.
Just another day, son,
in the as normal pose,
with heart on high alert
for something new to hope for.

**_*

So many moments to work out that I cannot
contain or remain
            in one. So I'll just have to wait
for another.

I won't have long.

**_*

Over there, on the horizon, between a blog of sunset
And a twitter of birdsong: Yes, it's true:

Humans!

They're walking around on the earth - they are -
as long as they can photograph each other

and post them for others

they'll survive. We can all rest
fatly in our beanbags
safe in this knowledge
and the truth constructed
in any renovation program.

* *

And there it was! Between family gatherings, marriages,
children, John Lennon's death, work and eating:

Your life! Waiting to be lived. You should've set your alarm.

\<If I had, it would have rung with this\>

All this   and death too.

* *

We should make landfall
by daybreak. But

let's stay here. In this life.
Come on, it'll be fine. It
already is. Let the wind
tell you it's true and agree
with the sun when it shines
an emblem on you. Pray
in person and despite metadata.

Throw a spanner in the search engine:

become an unGoogleable person,
always waiting to be discovered.
But never, ever ev—

***

Another day, another renovation program.

And it's time to admit that I
don't believe in the Great God
Poetry

just poetry/

/let the trees be my witness, or better, me theirs/

Will heaven care if I took care of my yard on Sundays?
Someone there will be sure to announce:

Remember the years without symbolism? And where the wind
was
the sun became? We had centuries

to solve this. And seconds to relive it.

***

At the train station, the evidence was clear: humans were
still running the place.

And

if the clapped out but not applauded jacarandas could sing

what would they sing of?

This is a new time? What's gone before is not?

But we know, don't we, that time has passed it
yet we're still just in time to say what should be said:

Stop your stupid singing, jacarandas!

{p.s. I don't even know if you're birds or trees}

**_*

The murmur of sex from the room next door. And the scrape of shovels.

v
v
v

==No, no, not yet, Man in Hooded Cloak With Scythe, they cry!
There's so much poetry we haven't read! Or re-read.
All these lives we haven't documented or stuffed up.
And then there's our sadness that Tom and Katie no longer talk. Will
we no longer make love nor talk? Tom jumped up and down
on the couch in love! But he's sleeping on his couch now,
dreaming of aliens. (Dreaming of them? Shuzbutt!! He is one.)

**_*

Smiling, A Juggler Spins His Batons
Those Instruments of Torture.

by T.T. Towers

Blah, blah, allah, etc. Bombings and bad asses.
Get the hell off our planet.*

* It's unclear who said that. The terrorist or the victim. Best to say
they said it for all of us. Sincerely, T.T. Towers.

_*

Some classes of vagrant are a-changin'. They talk to themselves
of start-ups. Various thankyous to the sun and rain and ASX100.
In death, they add, there will be no more
inexpensive soap pump packs
displayed outside chemists.

So clean up your act.

_*

The whoopee cushion I placed under the weight of what really
matters

has gone ahead and exploded! Well, pay me double!

And, I discover, it's good to exercise and it's good to pray and it's
good to say these things are good:

All this   and

everything, everywhere
made a comeback and recapped. So much

of everything all the time that every night
I saw it I thought the same thing:

Groundhog Day was the best film ever made
without a sequel.

_*_

Those days when we were apes scraping around on the floorboards
that only the inner ape could see . . .

. . . don't tell me your problems: I woke up in a Murakami novel,
the one where a man is trapped in a mine shaft for years! The sun
lighting him once a day. It led me to wonder:

If I were a bird, would I be the air I breathe?
If I were a fish, would I be the water I was out of?
If I was a bear . . . well, I know
it would be shit in the woods.

_*_

Various drunken Utopias. And Updates.
Did you read the last one?
You and I belong together
on a forty-foot twelve-step ladder, swaying
in the breeze.

There's no net. I repeat. There's no

_*_

Do you remember life? Wow,
        that was weird!

**_*

We're still waiting for something amazing to happen. Something
amazing will definitely happen. Somewhere. If something
amazing
happens in a forest is anybody there?

Ah well, there's always poetry: what else is it there for
but to open its wings and cover me. Thanks

      for the smell of feathers.

And this day. The same as any other. I wish it would
last forever, like last time.

**_*

Thank God! I missed the latest opportunity!
But, then again, what if the old days
were actually better?

For instance:

Last night, I rehearsed what I'd do today. Today
I'm doing it. I'm looking forward to tonight

And this:

      I opened the morning prayers:
          We'll just have to hope for the best, they said,
the decaying of the skin
      and burying of bones
         is not as disappointing as it seems.

Ah, universe, don't blank stare me like that. Surely your endless starfields can find room for another low-level disembodied consciousness?

** *
‾

The trouble with authenticity, he told me, is you can fake it.

And then the real truth: it's all go go go. Until we have to stop.
Permanently.

All this and . . .

a sweetness the air forgot to release.

Later, we all stood beneath the family wonder wall
and worried. Who would be next to be forgotten?

And we read together aloud, The Adventures of the Nowhere Brothers.
** *
‾

Be the change etc. you want to be etc. in the world etc.
--------after you've seen all the evil. Yeah, go ahead,
try it and see how you go!

(Well, thank you monkey brain for overriding lizard
on your way to plastic.)

And so, after all that science, I go to the dark place. Where nothing is.
Where I can concentrate on emptiness. And remember the sounds.
The scratching made on the cavern walls. There they are again.

** *
‾

"Be so alive in the world that people know who they are by what they see
you do" – (unknown, but possibly me.)

After that, no joke, someone ordered a decaf skinny cappuccino
with two sugars.

***

You couldn't call it a year, let alone a lisp. There's no further
need for the crisis talks now the car crash has come. I can
only let go of my own thoughts and so let loose a nightmare:

all the comments
on my social media posts
became my obituary.

Warning:

If death can get my grandma it can get you too.

So listen hyperbolically to the Big Note: it's played to make you
feel
unworthy of any music, even the perfect tune of your soul. Well,
especially
the tune of your soul. Because if you found out you were perfect
as you are
you wouldn't need to hear the Big Note.

(Yes, the secret: Big Noters are really small foolscappers)

***

My lover tells me she loves and appreciates me.
There's nowhere else she'd rather be.
Now I sing Hall and Oates songs. Without irony.
And I don't want the day to end and I notice that it hasn't.

v

v

v

v

And I don't want to go. I want to stay. I want to be here with everyone
forever. Even the bad ones. Even if I'm one of them. I want to stay
and eat and sleep and read. I don't want endless nothing with nobody
and no one. I want all the myths and dreams and hopes and theologies
and fairytales to be true. I want happy ever hereafter and I don't care
who's there and I'm happy to have the broom closet in one of the many
mansions' servant quarters with the smell of cat poo so long as there's
someone to talk to, a loaf of bread and the faintest memory of love. This
other thing, endless dark with nothing to do?

It can go to hell.

** *
—

This is the golden age of indifference. But I hope
someone holds up a lantern

on the lighted night path
my son wonders if he can step on his shadow. He can't see mine
stepping on me or the night slowly falling.

I feel like I'm speaking to the air. But I've said that before. To the air.

Little moments stripped from the big one.
Some guy told me he was going to die. Yeah, he said, I'm going to ground
for a while! I gave him what he wanted. A faithful laugh.

What are the brave, I thought, when fortune doesn't favour them?
The stupid.

I keep asking my wife do you think the world will ever get any better?
And she keeps offering me no reply. So it seems pointless
to protest that when I was a boy I didn't know I was, and now I'm a man
I never realised I'd be able to look at the boy from here, which is,
of course, now.

The boy looks up from the bed where he's chewed the AA battery
and his parents and grandparents have told him he's going to die
and he's beginning to accept it because they've forgotten to tell him

   they were joking. Oh boy

you haven't died! I'm here with you then as I was now.

All this and . . .

** *
—

Indian Mynah birds, it's known, are a pest species. And yet
on powerline music bars, in fresh custard winter sky,
their shapes still form a tune. But I don't read music
so I can't play along. They're gone before
I can call my music-reading son to tinkle the mynahs'

unwanted song on his second-hand piano.
He plays me invisible birds instead.

**_*

I am the adult from within which the child's watching.
Neither of us
can believe our eyes.

And here I am. And there's nowhere else. I'm where I am
because of what is, not what was or what might be. In this now
is everything. What I let go now I let go always.
Oh, but, by the way

sorry death, I'm not complying; I'm a refusenik forever. Again, I
apologise.

seventytimeseven

**_*

How about a wave that remains unsurfed,
unphotographed, alone, breaking and

wow: another human life. This one's mine!
And not enough time to make notes towards a poem
in response to Ecclesiastes.

So

Meditation was the process I used to stop writing. It didn't work.

Why so? What do you know
of my silence, or I of yours? Or either of us
of the great silence in which ours dwell?

No answer from you?

Then none from me.

** *
—

A
nother night
A
nother TV series that I'm
A
nother
episode further behind on.

** *
—

Two things of which we can be sure: the human heart
won't follow orders, and the world should be ruled by people
who don't think they rule the world.

** *
—

Good. I have nothing. I have everything I need.

These moments, these ones, even these from shopping list to
fridge,
are the ones between birth and old age, parents' deaths and your
own,

thrust upon your children.   O, let the chasm be filled

not with darkness
            nor desert

but wide open blue skies, flower blooms and that river called life

            running free
                        of bloated bodies
carcasses
                        or the fear that we may
even for a moment

be bones upon the banks.

All this. And a Brand New Episode: What I Always Was
I Remained and Became.

** *
—

A warm body beside me and a familiar sleeping face. The earth
begins a slow turn on its axis and I accept this like the drip
from the bathroom tap that will remain when the house is gone,
the street with it, and the city's whirlwind of lost opportunity.
The warm body beside me sleeps. I get up and tighten   the tap.

** *
—

Childhood has gone. It should be obvious enough that there's no way
to get it back. It seemed all we'd need to do was think hard enough
or remember long enough. And there we'd be: on our beds listening
to the radio, the rabbit outside in its cage still moments from forcing

its head
into a hole in the wire too small to pass through. But childhood
has gone.
And no one's pulling a rabbit out of anything.

Yet, still

that photo of me as a six-month-old. Sepia. Open-mouthed smile.

And from her funeral order of service photo, my grandmother
says
how happy I made everyone

every day. This day? I didn't get eaten by a lion in an
amphitheatre
which I'd once have taken as proof of my faithlessness, but now I
take
as a sign it's time to get some sleep.

** *
—

I spent too long thinking about having open heart surgery
on local anaesthetic, too long thinking about being allowed to
touch
my own heart, too long wondering for how many more days
it'd keep beating for me to realise it's beautiful and muscly sacred
with chambers warm as cathedral crypts lit by open fires.
That's when I decided to sit down beside it and strum my guitar.

** *
—

I know! Let's have a post-resurrection
after party! I'll bring the blues. You
bring the fool. We'll

dance as, well, you choose:

sunsets? blood oranges?
ghosts smoking cigarettes in the graveyard?

[Any dream will do.]

**_*

On the inner journey
there's no measure
of distance. There's
no space for space
and no time, of course, for ticking
off all our mistakes.

There are barriers
and witches' hats.
They're self-positioned
yet we don't know
when they'll appear.

There's no destination
and the journey's only part
of the journey. Deep is
another word for hello
and gates are only
gates when they're open.

If a tree falls in the forest
you know you've yet to
start the journey. And
if you hear it you'll know

the journey's finished
with you, and now
you are the journey.

**_ *

So difficult to clean
my teeth while wondering
if we're all just flashes of light
between two dark poles. Even
my son who hopes one day
to be a grandfather.

Note to him, my daughter and my other son:

One day you'll get to join
in with everything that's
going on till you learn
there's nothing going on
and then the joining in
really begins. And, especially
if you don't know where to get one,
send me a postcard from there.

**_ *

Yippee! The sights are the sounds in my sunglasses!
Give papa a wave, that's a good boy, that's what

the planet's saying, laughing
silently at something somebody was saying all through spring and
summer.

Sometimes to name the dream is enough
everything's been done and is being done and recorded
written about and discussed.   And there's no end to this.
So jump aboard or drown

or just sit down quietly in a corner!

(Secret additional clause):

I don't know a lot
but I know enough to know
that knowing a lot
isn't everything.

**_*

I live again this morning alive again this morning
the roadside trees aren't speaking but neither
are they travelling. They've nothing to say

beyond this:

Look at you, idiot, trying to interpret us!

Ha, ha, chuckle, chuckle, leaf rustle.

Things not going to plan? they say.

Then stop making plans.

** *
‾

A fool and his time to write
poetry are soon parted.

I have nothing to tell the world
anymore. It knows everything.

So go and airbrush your teeth. That's a good boy.

** *
‾

I spent a lot of time trying to care about things I didn't
care about. So now I know it and don't care
does that mean I did something right? Or am I just so so wrong?

Probably paradoxically both and.

I'll let the wind come, then the rain . . . Don't forget
the sun, it can come too! It'll be a party to remember.
We'll dance inside the tree trunks and shimmy in the leaves.
We'll shake the drops from ourselves and claim the dry
as our own, the whole in the hole of the desert!

So far from the truth of myself — the warmth of the way plant
life grows
on my imagination and takes me back to a time I never had.

** *
‾

Out of the suburbs this way something remarkable comes. It looks

like
Shakespeare riding a wheelie bin, or maybe Cervantes eating
a Bunnings sausage with one ear on the race call and the other
on his child's cry for McDonald's. Out of the suburbs this way
something remarkable comes, pointing at each face of the moon
as if Janus were yet to be born, while taking another child to ballet
practice
where the suburbs whirlpool and the tornado of dishwashing subsides,
you see him holding a sparkler out front of his porch crying for the days
when Midas touched him, and out of the suburbs he came, gold-capped
fillings shining biting into some other smart heart's hamburger.

** *
—

Theological lesson when I woke up
via still small voice in the centre
of my soul or something:

It doesn't matter what you call the Unknowable,
it matters what the Unknowable calls you.

And remember before you go to sleep tonight:

there are millions of people around the world singing.
Then ask yourself: why can't I hear them?

** *
—

The simple things in life are often our deaths. As simple as watching
a blue bull ant's shell shine in the morning sun. Is it your time or his?

When Patrick Swayze shouted as a ghost in Ghost, "I had a life!"
he was, you must know, speaking for all of us.

***

Death has a government face:

shiny, nose upturned, a voice that speaks
the answers before you hear a sound.

And there's not some great ending
or beginning. There's only the
turning of the planet and everything
science knows about how the sun
doesn't go down but burns out.
To say that's how it is for us would be
to say our lives and eyes are something like the sun.
And I think we've heard enough of that for one
cycle of the earth through space.

Notes

'More Skills for Living', 'Central Questions' and 'Enlightenment', first published *Arena*.

'Psalm 19b' and 'Letter to Franz Kafka' first published *Cordite*.

'The Sun Moved to a Supplementary Position', first published, *Plumwood Mountain*.

'Funereal' first published *Westerly*.

'First Day of Holidays', first published *Studio* and won the Studio Poetry Prize.

'The Birth of Sophia', first published *Studio*.

'Weekend Warriors of the Apocalypse', first published *Australian Poetry Journal*.

'Portrait of Departure', first published *Antipodes: American Journal of Australian Literature*.

'Sermon on the Institution', first published *Eureka Street*.

'Process Theology (a-c)' first published *Imagination in an Age of Crisis* (Wipf & Stock).

'Inception', 'Marking Mark's Discovery' and 'Portrait of What Came Next', first published *Social Alternatives*.

'And That's the Over', first published *Meniscus*.

'Three on the Tree', first published, *Blue Pepper*.

'Koans for the Young' appeared as text with an accompanying film clip on *Litpoetry* podcast's YouTube channel.

Sections of 'Song in the Key of Beginner's Mind' appeared as lyrics and poems on the album *My Coffin Lid, My Shield* (2019) by Paul Mitchell and Simon Mason.

Acknowledgments

Thank you to David Musgrave and the team at Puncher and Wattmann for publishing this work and for your support and encouragement. A special thanks to Ross Gillett for your careful edit of the manuscript.

Thanks also to Kevin Brophy, Nathan Curnow, and alicia sometimes for your thoughtful feedback on poems in this collection.

Thank you Fleur Rendell for allowing me to use your wonderful work, *Tinderbox Tree* (2009), on the cover (fleurrendell.com). And a big thanks to the editors of the publications in which some of the poems in this collection first appeared: *Antipodes*; *Arena*; *Australian Poetry Journal*; *Blue Pepper*; *Cordite*; *Eureka Street*; *Imagination in an Age of Crisis* (Wipf & Stock); *Litpoetry*; *Meniscus; Plumwood Mountain; Social Alternatives; Studio;* and *Westerly.*

Biography

Paul Mitchell has published seven books, including a novel, *We. Are. Family.* (MidnightSun Publishing, 2016) and four poetry collections. His poems, essays, and stories have appeared over the last twenty-five years in publications such as The Age, The Australian, Antipodes (US), Best Australian Stories and Poems, Cordite, Griffith Review, The Guardian, Heat, Island, Meanjin, Overland, Rolling Stone, and Westerly. He has won, been placed or commended in many literary prizes and has developed several works for stage and screen, including co-writing the documentary Actions to Live By for the AFL, which covered the Brisbane Lions' 2001-2003 dynasty. La Mama Theatre (Melbourne) has accepted his play, You're the Man, for a two-week season in 2025. In 2023, Paul and Simon Mason performed their poetry-meets-music album, *My Coffin Lid, My Shield* at Denmark Festival of Voice (WA) and Sonic Poetry Festival, Melbourne.